MASTER YOUR MIND

10 Tips to Shift Your Mindset

DEDICATION

*This book is dedicated to everyone that has
blessed me with their presence and wisdom.
Thank you for taking the time to educate me and
help me understand the value of life.*

CONTENTS

PREFACE

Growing up in Little Rock, AR, it was hard for me to envision myself as a future transformational speaker, real estate investor, entrepreneur, and role model before I eventually achieved all of those things. See, everyone has a path, dream, and purpose; it is our job to believe that what we want from life is attainable.

Starting out in 2020, I embarked on the difficult path of pursuing my goals on my own. I had to figure things out for myself, flailing and fumbling as I went along. Flying solo made my journey ten times harder than it had to be. One of the biggest challenges I faced wasn't only my lack of resources… it was my failure to believe in myself. Hear me out: You do not have to make the same mistakes I did. I've gone through the fire, so in some instances, you do not have to. The result is this book, intended not only as a guide to help you avoid the pitfalls I fell into, but it's also a glimpse into the personal experiences I encountered while overthinking the process. I am Terryl Humphrey, and I'm here to teach you how to *"Learn as you go and grow as you learn!"*

TIP 1

Find Your "*Why*"

It took me years to understand that self-aware-ness means investing time in myself, identify-ing my flaws, and recognizing my attributes. Once I embraced that awareness, my eyes were opened to everything I'd suppressed within myself. Begin-ning with my childhood.

I grew up in a single-parent household, where my mother taught my two brothers and me how to believe in our dreams and go all out for them.

Our situation was difficult; however, everything we desire--even when it's hard, is worth pursuing. For example, playing football my entire life birthed the drive and determination I still thrive on today. Football taught me how to push and persevere. Pushing isn't always so easy to do when times get tough, but it molds us into a new version of ourselves. Specifically with regard to football, weathering the grueling practices, inclement weather, tedious classwork, and injuries made me a better player and person.

Because football is a team sport, every person must do their job both on and off the field in order to be successful. And I mean everyone: coaches, players, trainers – all of us. I wish that back then, I'd grasped the concept that the entire team collectively contributes to wins and losses. But I was naïve and just didn't get it. As an adult, I can say with the utmost confidence that I now fully understand a team's dynamic and how it works.

Little Rock Central High School is where my life and purpose were formed in subconscious before I was fully aware of what was going on. During my sophomore year, I observed two teammates working their butts off to improve every day, both on and off the field. Their determination to be the best linebackers at any cost was evident in their work ethic. Coupled with their belief in themselves, I realized I could achieve the same level of greatness as long as I was dedicated to my craft.

Inspired by my classmates, I became obsessed with having a better year than my 10th-grade season. I was yelled at for messing up drills, supported my teammates even when I was benched, was con-stantly conditioning (training) with extra work-outs, and studied our game films to advance the way I needed to. I endured it all. But I knew that's what it would take in order for us to be successful together. My fierce focus earned me a starting line-backer position--the best reward I'd ever received. What did I learn from all that work? Success isn't easy, but exercising the will to push through the hard times eventually pays off.

My focus wasn't about me, it was about the team. Prior to my junior year, I was selfish and didn't bother honing my craft; I wasn't a great player at all. Once I shifted my mindset and focus to improving myself for the team, my value increased. I became a leader and helped others grow as I had done. Today, I am the person I am solely because I worked on myself for the sake of the team.

My *"why"* is helping others transform their mindset to become the best version of themselves. To instill faith and confidence in my clients through persistence, creating our own narrative of success. Again, I lead by example, pursuing my goals while being transparent with those I mentor, publicly displaying the good and the bad. One way to determine your *why* is by identifying your trauma. Once you define the root, it will show you the reason. Your *why* is the pain that you have experienced and gives you the credibility to share your story with the next person.

The discomfort of not having my father in my life as a child is the trauma that led to my *why*.

For years, I was lost, grasping to discover my identity, forced to learn how to be a man on my own. My negative mindset and lack of confidence caused me to stumble often along my journey; however, I learned that my purpose is instilling faith and confidence in others, and to help them not faint along their journey. This assistance was something I didn't have growing up, but I found a way to repurpose my pain to fulfill my purpose.

Master Your Mind: Understanding your *why* shapes your outlook on life, including how you see the world, yourself, and others. Your *why* ultimately helps you live intentionally and with purpose.

What is your WHY? Think about who, what, how, and your purpose.

_____

_____

_____

_____

_____

_____

_____

_____

_____

_____

_____

_____

_____

_____

Master Your Mind

_____

_____

_____

_____

_____

_____

_____

_____

_____

_____

_____

_____

_____

_____

_____

_____

_____

_____

_____

Thinking big opens the door to making it happen. If it is easy to accomplish, we are thinking too small.

TIP 2

Repurpose Your Pain

The pain I experienced was the gateway to success for me because I was forced to learn more about my past, accept who I was, and who I am becoming.

During my senior year in high school, I tore my ACL and a part of my meniscus in my right knee during the season's fourth football game. I was devastated! Since the death of my grandmother in 2009, it was only the second time in my life I'd experienced a tragic situation of that magnitude. I'd never suffered a major injury in my football career-- much less my life. Yet, this accident ended my high school sports career.

Watching all of my hard work go down the drain in such a horrific way left me speechless. What hurt the most was not being able to play alongside my teammates--my family, ever again. The physical pain had nothing on the mental and emotional toll it took on myself and the team. The season started off well, but we ended with a dismal 3-7 record... the same as the previous season.

Senior year was more special than any other season because it was my final year playing the sport I loved. I loved how the guys and I came together in unity through long practices, hot days, times when we didn't want to condition, film reviews, and Saturday practices. Then there were the days we just chilled. At the forefront for all of us was the importance of building success together, rather than accomplishing small wins individually. It shouldn't have surprised anyone when my injury caused me to miss the grind with my football family so much that I isolated myself.

There's always a lesson behind the pain; we just have to learn how to identify it. The lesson the excruciating pain of losing my high school football career taught me was the importance of having the right people around you. Sometimes, what we go through helps us grow through it. Surrounding ourselves with people who have the same drive and determination to be great that we do, is a reflection of our need for each other.

Having the right people in my life outside of sports became vital for me. The growth I received from having the right tribe caused me to become more aware of myself, my values, and my needs. Through the process, I learned the art of patience and the value it holds. It took me a long time to find myself, before I did, I had no clue who I was looking for. The search for me was a journey within itself, one that led me to join the Marine Corps. Military life brought out the leadership skills I never knew existed within me; it was uncomfortable but enabled me to repurpose myself.

Master Your Mind: Repurpose your pain. Acknowledge and accept that the pain is attached to your purpose.

How can you repurpose your pain to fulfill your purpose?

_____

_____

_____

_____

_____

_____

_____

_____

_____

_____

_____

_____

_____

_____

_____

_____

_____

_____

_____

_____

_____

_____

_____

_____

_____

_____

_____

_____

_____

_____

_____

Always be a good person with healthy boundaries. Being too nice allows people to take advantage of your good heart, and you'll wind up taking a heartbreaking loss.

TIP 3

Discipline is the Key to Success

Discipline forces us to break old habits and helps us to better ourselves. For example, I really dislike working out. Putting myself through unbearable pain and discomfort to maintain a proper healthy lifestyle seems irrational to me. However, I understand that discomfort gives birth to growth. Working out during my football years boosted my confidence to face any and everybody on the opposing team, no matter how strong they appeared. When the game was taken away from me, my motivation for the daily workouts went with it. At least, I thought it did.

Once the reason I thought I had to be disciplined disappeared, I saw that working out did more than get me in shape and help me maintain a healthy lifestyle. It helped me see the possibility of attaining the success I dreamed of; however, I had to unlearn the bad habits I'd amassed in order to create a better life for myself.

Implementing new, healthy habits meant putting my knowledge and education to use. There had been so many times I flew blind without the benefit of my "why," until the reason revealed itself much later. That's why I love football so much--the lessons are easily transferable from sports to mainstream life. The success of the *play* is in the small details; *life's* details determine the amount of that success we'll achieve.

Life's what we make it, and no matter how hard we try, we can't control the outcome. This keeps me from worrying about the end result of a situation because I know the preparation and execution I put into it determines the outcome I will arrive at. See, when I began preparing myself for future success, I learned I had a lot of work to do if I was ever going to see it. Educating myself, creating discipline in every aspect of my life, and most importantly, embracing the journey were all a part of helping me get to the end game.

Master Your Mind: Nothing happens without discipline. It starts with your mind; whether positive or negative, your thoughts dictate your actions and results.

How will becoming more disciplined help you achieve success?

_____

_____

_____

_____

_____

_____

_____

_____

_____

_____

_____

_____

_____

_____

Master Your Mind

_____

_____

_____

_____

_____

_____

_____

_____

_____

_____

_____

_____

_____

_____

_____

_____

_____

_____

Cut off limitations. Self-doubt is the major distraction that limits what we're able to accomplish if we're not focused.

TIP 4

Believe in Yourself

It takes the right people, conversation, and the perfect moment to believe what we can't see.

Years ago, I failed to see the power of believing in myself. My injury catapulted me into a state of complacency; my content mindset lacked confidence. Finally, I decided to get mentors who were successful in my chosen field to help me regain it. Mike and Steve--my mentors--taught me how real estate works, and the elements to be successful in that arena, as well as applying the principles to my life outside of work.

Working in real estate requires confidence, assertiveness, and faith in self. Working alongside my mentors has taught me so much--for example, the art of listening more than speaking. Having an attentive ear allows me to identify whether there's a problem that needs to be fixed, or if we are compatible to work together. I also learned that sales is about solving our customers' problems and alleviating stress. Eventually, listening became a solid skill that helped me tend to my customers' needs and successfully utilize the sale to solve their problems.

Growing up, I had no idea what the sales industry was, or why it even mattered. Now, I can tell you that sales is about presenting a solution for a specific problem, at the perfect time. For instance, in real estate, some homeowners sell their houses due to some kind of distress that has taken place. (Divorce, pre-foreclosure, absentee owner, the desire to relocate, etc.). There are many reasons why people choose to sell their homes. As the salesman (*problem solver*), it is my job to understand why they are considering putting their home on the market and how I may assist.

Learning sales as problem-solving from the ground up wasn't an easy task, especially having no experience in the field. Thankfully, my mentors took me under their wings, teaching me how to find my voice and implement the lessons they taught me. Similar to football coaches, Mike and Steve taught me the game; however, it was up to me to apply the lessons, perfect them, and score. It definitely took time, but the only person who could make a difference for me, was me. After a while, I saw that I wasn't bringing as much value to Mike and Steve as I would've liked, so I stepped away from their business to further my education and get a true grasp on the meaning of selling.

Sales occur every day, even when we are unaware there are transactions taking place. In my case, I wasn't doing the selling--I was being sold. Picture this: Every time I go to the store, I leave with my purchases, and the store keeps my money in exchange for the goods. In real estate, by learning to close on a home properly, I was the person exchanging value for currency, monetizing my craft. If you are unfamiliar with sales and the purpose of closing, I'll refer you to *The Closers Survival Guide*, written by Grant Cardone. There is much to be learned from this book that you can apply.

My weak confidence was strengthened by consulting with my mentors and perfecting my craft outside of football. The stronger my confidence became, the more I started believing in myself. My confidence was boosted because of my experience, education, and refusal to give up. Slowly, it became second nature to celebrate my small wins and how far I'd come. It was hard, which meant only the strong would survive, and I'm still standing more confidently than ever.

Master Your Mind: Believe in yourself. Once you truly believe in yourself, nothing or NO THING is impossible for you to achieve! Operating from a growth mindset, you know that with confidence, hard work, and practice, you can achieve any and everything.

With full confidence in yourself and your abilities, what opportunities or possibilities would you pursue?

_____

_____

_____

_____

_____

_____

_____

_____

_____

_____

_____

_____

_____

Master Your Mind

Believe you can, and you shall. Always implore faith, and you'll receive the best results with time and the right effort.

TIP 5

Just Start

Never let the fear of failure outweigh the possibility of succeeding. Stop allowing fear to control and stagnate you--just start where you are.

For a long time, I let fear control who I was, which affected my identity. Back in 2018, when I started the journey to self-discovery, I was pursuing a purpose without knowing the "why" behind it. My answer came in the form of joining the United States Marine Corps. I enlisted as a way out of complacency and to develop my work skills--a mechanic, specifically. So, my brother Flex and I left for boot camp on one of the most rewarding experiences I've had in my life.

I'm grateful I didn't have to deal with boot camp, school, and MCT (Marine Combat Training) alone. Flex had my back no matter what, and I had his. The Marines are a brotherhood, just like football teams are family. Sometimes, our differences cause us to grow closer. Getting off the plane at the USO (*United Services Organizations*) was scary; I had no idea what to expect. Fear of the unknown triggered panic attacks in me, making the situation worse than it was. I was filled with anxiety, constantly overthinking and telling myself that I wasn't good enough. But having Flex on the journey with me helped me to withstand it all.

People join the military for their own personal reasons. Family tradition, the desire to serve the country, or having nowhere else to go are all reasons I've heard. Whatever the case, every reason is valid, and I had to learn that was okay.

My older brother enlisted in the army; however, it wasn't a good fit for him. He actually participated in JROTC (Junior Officer Training Corps.), so he knew what to expect before reporting for service. I didn't have the same advantage of prior experience as my brother had, which made military life foreign to me, but I made it. In football, I was used to working as a team to win games, but the marines had a higher calling to defend our country. I wanted more for myself; enlisting was my way of achieving it. In the interim, I was forced to leave my comfort zone and enter into the unknown to figure out who I was.

One of the main components military training stressed was the importance of always looking presentable. It took almost the entire duration of my military career to understand why. The scariest part wasn't adjusting; it was that it took more than four years for me to fully understand the lessons I was supposed to learn. What the United States Marine Corps taught me is much bigger than myself; we come together to serve and make a difference in others' lives.

I'll admit my selfish intentions for enlisting (like escaping my hometown in order to put myself first) led me to misunderstand the importance of serving. I failed to comprehend the mission until the mission was almost over. I wasn't ready to accept military discipline; however, I realize how valuable that discipline has been to my present and future.

My goal is to educate the masses on the opportunities out here in the world to create the life they've only dreamed of. Sustainable living takes exposure to knowledge and experience, and patience. We can't and do not have to attain success alone--this is why I am sharing my journey with you. Starting out, you won't have all the answers, but getting started is half the battle. Trial and error will help you figure out the steps along the path to greatness.

Master Your Mind: Just start. Don't overthink and delay the process. Start where you are, and grow from there.

What does letting go and getting started look like to you?

_____

_____

_____

_____

_____

_____

_____

_____

_____

_____

_____

_____

_____

_____

Master Your Mind

_____

_____

_____

_____

_____

_____

_____

_____

_____

_____

_____

_____

_____

_____

_____

_____

_____

Time is of the essence, so we must work with the time that we have.

TIP 6

Be Determined to Succeed

While on my journey, I have learned that my success is my responsibility and no one else's. It takes time to develop this level of awareness; nonetheless, I had to accept it. My goal was to bring value to things without first understanding what I had to offer. Until I learned what I possessed inside, I wandered aimlessly in my pursuit. I was essentially preaching without practicing what I was speaking about.

In 2020, I was determined to figure out who I was but didn't know where to start. By August of that year, I launched my real estate career, fully persuaded that I would be a millionaire by September--one month after I began. So, there were a couple of important lessons I was taught here: There's no such thing as overnight success, the right education leads to the life I desire, I dream big, and I really believe in myself more than I thought I did.

Getting started and messing up is better than prolonging an already lengthy journey. In other words, any action is better than taking none at all. One of the first mindset books I read was, *Rich Dad Poor Dad* by Robert Kiyosaki. The book has little to do with real estate; however, it helps people transform the way they perceive life. For example, an impoverished mindset indicates that we're thinking too small, with limited intention and action.

Conversely, a rich mindset dreams big and goes hard or goes home. *Rich Dad Poor Dad* is a powerful read because it details varying perspectives that shape how people think. Being exposed to a new level of thought by reading this book, I was compelled to believe that I'd achieve millionaire status in a month's time, simply because I was exposed to expanding my mind.

Also, bearing witness to the success hard work produced for others helped me dream bigger than I had before. If they could do it, so could I. Every day, I think about the kind of success I want and how to make it a reality. In full disclosure, I'm still figuring out what success looks like; however, I've identified key components to help me get there. First of all, money is a reward, whereas the journey and the lessons demonstrated who I needed to become. The new version I see of myself requires that I implement discipline and diligence to achieve my goals. At times it's overwhelming, difficult, and time-consuming, but I always see it as achievable.

When you take the time to educate yourself and execute your plans, no matter how imperfect, the hard tasks eventually become easy, and you improve as you go along. I am beyond blessed and thankful that I met Mike and Steve because they gave me an understanding of what a good business consists of. They drilled in me that good businesses solve problems and, most importantly, never take advantage of the customers they serve. My mother (whom I affectionately call Vetty Vet) instilled in me the value of treating people right. Vetty Vet cares so much for people she often forgets to care for herself. This is a good and bad trait to have, simply because being too nice opens the door for people to take advantage of her. However, having a balance between both creates boundaries.

I'm proud to bear many of my mother's traits: being a good person and striving to attain knowledge are a couple of them. I'm also as understanding as my mother, and most importantly, we thrive seeing other people succeed. Success is giving back and helping while we succeed together. My brave mother was surviving for our family, not just for herself. Often, we tend to do things out of love, but we have to put ourselves first--everyone else's needs will be met after we're taken care of. We can't be any good for anyone else if we're no good for ourselves.

Success for me is envisioning the lifestyle I want to create for myself. I want to give back but can't give what I don't have to offer. I am determined to see my goals through; I have a burning desire that my dreams will come to fruition, no matter what.

Master Your Mind: Be determined. Your success depends on you, your determination, and level of commitment. Be committed to succeed and do it!

What steps are you willing to take to achieve the success you desire?

_____

_____

_____

_____

_____

_____

_____

_____

_____

_____

_____

_____

_____

_____

_____

_____

_____

_____

_____

_____

_____

_____

_____

_____

_____

_____

_____

_____

_____

_____

_____

_____

Celebrate your small wins in order to recognize your growth.

TIP 7

Become a Student of Life

Life has a funny way of teaching us lessons that are beneficial for our future success. Taking heed requires understanding, will, awareness, and, most importantly, the desire to heal. Trauma doesn't heal by itself; however, once we work to deal with and move past the pain, we heal.

In hindsight, my mother did a fantastic job raising three boys by herself. Knowing what I know now, I realize how hard it was for Vetty Vet, even though she made it appear easy. Trauma has been the most difficult emotion for me to overcome because I was the one that had to deal with it. The lessons I learned when I was younger helped with other problems I went through, such as my divorce. Sometimes, pain truly is the best teacher to learn from.

Pain taught me how to stop overlooking my emotions. I loved my ex-wife; when it was time for us to part ways, my heart was shattered into many pieces. Those pieces were everything I needed to help me grow. For instance, I needed to learn how to communicate how I was feeling and why. Communication is imperative in any relationship, whether that relationship be romantic, friendship, business, or otherwise.

The next most important lesson was to love myself. This proved difficult for me, and I wasn't sure where to start. Self-love is a confidence builder that displays the amount of belief we have in ourselves. It's hard to love people when we don't love the person we see in the mirror daily.

Growth means dealing with overwhelming circumstances. I came to the conclusion that I wasn't the only one experiencing hardship. I was growing through a divorce; however, others around me were dealing with something similar, like separating from their partners.

Connecting with others who understood my struggles showed me that I was going to make it through the fire okay. The thing about being *okay* is that it takes time to heal before the new you emerges. My pain wasn't the end of the world, but it did teach me more about who I was and who I was becoming. The person I am today is because of the time and effort I invested in working on myself.

In order to find yourself, find a way to manage the pain and relieve your mind of the trauma you've internalized. As incredible as she is, my mother didn't guide me through expressing my feelings, which caused me to learn how to work around them rather than confront how I felt. Being in touch with my emotions opened me to the parts of myself I wasn't familiar with. It takes time, but the time you spend investing in yourself is a reflection of how you perceive life.

Master Your Mind: Become a student of life. Life's lessons are meant to broaden and expand your thinking. Whether good or bad, use those experiences as lessons to catapult you into your destiny.

What are some life situations, circumstances, and lessons that have shaped the way you think?

_____

_____

_____

_____

_____

_____

_____

_____

_____

_____

_____

_____

_____

_____

Master Your Mind

_____

_____

_____

_____

_____

_____

_____

_____

_____

_____

_____

_____

_____

_____

_____

_____

_____

_____

Educate yourself and invest time in achieving your goals. It takes self-awareness and willingness to learn more about yourself.

TIP 8

Own Your Deficiencies

Our biggest critic is the person in the mirror.

The song *Man in the Mirror* (Michael Jackson) really hits home for me. Wanting to make a change meant changing who I was first. The impact I want to leave behind is bigger than me; however, if I don't work on my deficiencies, there will always be something that stops me: the main roadblock being lack of confidence in what I bring to the table.

The thing about confidence is that it fluctuates. Some days, we're more confident than others. We can also be strongly confident in some areas while weak in others. Finding the strength to boost our confidence to an even keel is important. I boosted myself by furthering my education, becoming well-versed, and believing in what I was presenting. Confidence on the football field had been easy because I put the time into perfecting my craft. By senior year, my confidence was through the roof. In fact, I was super confident. Then my injury occurred.

One of the devastating effects of tearing my ACL was feeling like all of my hard work was a waste of time and everything I worked for was cruelly stripped from me. My confidence was shattered; without football, I no longer had a reason or a purpose. At least, that's how I felt at the time. The good thing about confidence is that it can be rebuilt even after it's broken. I'm grateful my mentors helped restore that within me.

Life is difficult, but having experienced people around us helps us to thrive. Steve taught me the importance of finding my voice while learning how to adapt to my audience. It was a shock since I didn't know the first thing about business or how to present myself. Taking so long for it to click was embarrassing. I just didn't get it. So, Steve told me to study, and that's exactly what I did. Education is a key confidence builder. Lack of it makes life more complex, which causes confusion.

I knew education was vital; however, I was unaware of how every aspect of life involves some level of learning. One of my shortcomings was my lack of education in the professional field I was entering, so my confidence was adversely affected. My purpose is to educate the masses on the opportunities that come from belief within oneself. I must be confident in my ability to do it. We remediate our deficiencies by doing the work to acquire knowledge, understanding, and / or skills to add to our repertoire. Find a coach in your field who cares about you and is willing to tell you the truth about who you are and what you need to do in order to change and grow.

Master Your Mind: Own your deficiencies. A fixed, stubborn mindset says that you'll never be able to do something, but being open to growth says even though you may not be able to do it now, you'll eventually be able to.

Why is it important that we address our deficiencies?

_____

_____

_____

_____

_____

_____

_____

_____

_____

_____

_____

_____

_____

_____

_____

_____

_____

_____

_____

_____

_____

_____

_____

_____

_____

_____

_____

_____

_____

_____

_____

_____

_____

Focus on yourself to learn more about who you are.

TIP 9

Be Fearless

Fear is defined as "an unpleasant emotion caused by the belief that someone or something is dangerous, likely to cause pain or a threat." I love this definition because it breaks down how we, as people, overcomplicate the power of belief. Belief is an emotion that we often waste time putting in the wrong thing. Once I gained the confidence to ask my wife for a divorce, I believed that being single was going to be hard for me, which was why it took so long for me to make the move. After it was done, I realized divorce was the best option for me because it meant putting myself, my emotional health, and my well-being first.

I am not saying changing my views was easy, because it definitely wasn't. Nonetheless, the adjustment was necessary. Belief goes a long way--it drives us to keep pushing in spite of circumstances. I spent too much time pouring my energy into fear rather than faith, which is defined as, "complete trust or confidence in someone or something." It's amazing how the definition of both fear and faith are rooted in *belief*. People function off fear because it's easier to manage than positive thinking, which is a journey in itself. The power of belief taught me that all bad situations have some good within them. I just had to identify what that *good* was.

On June 29, 2022, I was in a terrible car accident that resulted in my 2013 Nissan Altima being totaled. The positive that came from the situation was that everyone involved in the accident emerged okay. The downfall was I lost my car. Today, my faith is stronger because the accident taught me that while I can't control what happens, I can control my response to it.

The bottom line is, I have more control over myself than anything. Control was something I lacked in the past because I didn't understand it. Now I equate control with awareness and a tangible demonstration of the level of growth we've accomplished. Having control strengthens the power of faith.

Life happens to everyone, yet the strength to respond in a positive manner shows how much growth has been developed.

Master Your Mind: Be Fearless. Exercise faith instead. Remember, fear and faith are both rooted in belief. CHOOSE what you believe!

What has fear prevented you from doing or pursuing? How will you take your power back?

_____

_____

_____

_____

_____

_____

_____

_____

_____

_____

_____

_____

_____

_____

_____

*You are valuable; no one can take that away
from you unless you give them control.*

TIP 10

Be Yourself

Without knowing who I was, it was impossible to be myself. Don't get me wrong, I caught glimpses of myself, but there was still so much to learn. We can be taught every aspect of life, depending on who's educating us. We need reliable sources to fill in the missing gaps; my sources were my environment and life itself, both of which taught me what I needed to get through the days as I got to know myself.

Coming to grips with who I am was overwhelming, to say the least. Life has a funny way of humbling us in the most random ways; however, life is the key indicator of self-awareness. The best lessons I've learned came from focusing on myself, rather than seeking them. Life taught me that I come first and everyone and everything comes next. Selfish is what it appears to be because it is not the norm; nonetheless, being selfish creates a selfless environment. I say this because once I know who I am, I can easily identify every emotion, attribute, and limitation I have. I am also able to identify who I don't mind being around and having a conversation with. I can converse with everyone, yet not everyone can have a conversation with me because I've become selective about who I allow access to me.

I don't stretch myself too thin or subject myself to circumstances and situations that I am uncomfortable with. Exposing who I really am gave me the ability to be myself. Now, I recognize my value, and I believe in myself more than anything or anyone. I've learned that belief comes from faith and faith from recognition. What we bring to the table must be developed from within. Skills, knowledge, interactions. It's all inside of us. Our value helps us to help others believe in themselves.

Misunderstandings follow the heels of lack of education, making the journey more difficult than it has to be. However, difficulty also creates resiliency. For me, resiliency strengthened my mentality because it prompted me to work on myself rather than against myself. In order to grow into a new version of yourself, start by identifying every positive and negative attribute you possess and work on these things instead of ignoring them.

Master Your Mind: As the saying goes, be yourself because everyone else is taken. More importantly, there's only one you and the world needs YOU.

Which 3 words sum up who you are as a person? What's the significance of each word?

Master Your Mind

Be true to yourself. Treat people how you want to be treated.

BONUS TIP

Have Fun

I am still learning how to have fun during self-discovery. It's not easy when you don't believe you deserve to have fun, and admittedly, it's done some damage to my mental health. So, in order to create balance, I've started listening to my intuition. When I feel overwhelmed, I try to relax. If I can't relax, I focus on happy distractions to ease my mind. Building a strong foundation takes hard work, which often leads to stress. Taking days off here and there is vital to relieving the stress we need to drop to make it through the upcoming days.

I'm proud of my journey. I've learned so much that has helped me identify my purpose and my gift. Having fun is a part of the journey, but it takes sacrifice to attain the life I desire, where I can do anything and enjoy life for what it is. Essentially, I'm taking control of my destiny. I'm at peace now, focusing on my growth and becoming the best version of myself. Now, I'm able to attract the type of life that brings fulfillment. Peace enables us to experience life in different, better, more exciting new ways as we grow and enjoy *living* as opposed to *existing*.

I sacrifice today for the things I want tomorrow. The process takes time, but time is all that we have. The best lessons always come at the right time. What I learn today is meant for years to come; many things we hear today are meant to be understood later. The day I realized this was when I was able to walk away from my unhappy marriage.

Learning to have fun has also taught me to celebrate my accomplishments. It's hard to understand that we deserve to have fun, but I'm able to deviate when it is time to have fun. Sacrifice today for the fun that will come after years of developing who you are as a person.

Master Your Mind: Fun fuels you. Take time out to enjoy some fun and get the fuel you need to move forward.

What do you enjoy doing for fun? How will you ensure that you do it more often?

_____

_____

_____

_____

_____

_____

_____

_____

_____

_____

_____

_____

_____

_____

_____

_____

_____

_____

_____

_____

_____

_____

_____

_____

_____

_____

_____

_____

_____

_____

_____

_____

EPILOGUE

Life is what you make it, but it starts with creating the vision you want for yourself. It will be challenging; however, investing time in yourself makes you stronger. Quitting is not an option; your success must work, no matter what! I wasn't able to think this way until I envisioned myself as successful--something I never pictured myself becoming until I wanted more for myself.

My mother, Vetty Vet, raised us to believe in ourselves and go for anything that we desired. Ultimately, we were operating out of a survival mindset instead of an abundance mindset. Remember the book I mentioned earlier--*Rich Dad Poor Dad*? It completely changed my point of view as I pursued my purpose. *Rich Dad Poor Dad* goes in-depth, exploring how the lives of two fathers (one rich, one poor) differentiated from each other. Keep in mind the "poor" father wasn't poor because of his status; *poor* is what we think--rich is who we become. The poor father was conservative and believed he couldn't afford much. By contrast, the rich father was a dreamer who went after what he wanted.

After reading this book, I became obsessed with achieving my goals. I packed my days watching podcasts, learning more about the elements of success, and unpacking everything that caused me to operate out of fear. I've discovered that the best way to find my purpose is to function off of faith instead of letting fear conquer me. The thing that became achievable was the power of belief--starting with leaving Little Rock behind to explore the opportunities out there waiting for me.

I've also adapted the mind to *pay it forward*. One of my most pressing, burning desires is to achieve billionaire status, so that I can help as many people as possible. Grant Cardone was the first billionaire I was exposed to; now, I view myself as a *billionaire in the making*.

Pain creates opportunities once it's recognized and confronted rather than making excuses for it. The pains I endured as a child and man have given birth to this book to help you change your mindset, future, and, ultimately, your life. I'm Terryl (with a "y")

Humphrey, signing off. If this book has helped you in some way, please recommend it to anyone who may need help with their personal development. Thank you, and I can't wait to hear your testimony of how you've mastered your mind!

ABOUT THE AUTHOR

Terryl Humphrey is an author, entrepreneur, and orator. Hailing from Little Rock, Arkansas, Terryl has dreams and aspirations of becoming a billionaire and impacting the lives of a billion people. His goal is to educate the masses about the limitless possibilities that exist. Terryl aspires to help others transform their mindset to become the best version of themselves. Through faith, confidence, and persistence he believes we can create our own narrative of success.